RUDE AND RIBALD
RACING RHYMES

RUDE AND RIBALD
RACING RHYMES

Compiled by Janet Benney

In aid of

THE SPINAL INJURIES ASSOCIATION

PATRON: H.R.H. THE PRINCESS ROYAL

76 St James's Lane, London N10 3DF Telephone: 01 444 2121

CONTRIBUTORS

Anon
Bill Armstrong

Geoff Baxter
Rip Bissill
Paul Benney
Ed Byrne
Kenneth Bright
Elliott Baker
William Bush
Mrs Gerald Benney
Andrew Bruce
Lady Barry
Jack Berry
Lt. Col. F.M. Beale
Mrs Ben Brooks
Peter Bromley
Aubrey Brabazon
Angela Bell
Julian Byng
Lord Ballantrae

Col. N. Cowley
Paul Cook
Mrs Peter Calver
Alex Csaky
Lord Carnarvon
John Carden, M.A.
Christopher Curtis
T.F.M. Corrie
Robin Christie
J.A. Campion
Dennis Clarke

N.J. Dent
Stan Dutson
Steven Duffy
Mrs John Dunlop
Martin Diggle

Hugh Ellis
Mick Easterby
Mrs H.N. Edwards
Chris Ellis

A.C. Frost
Jim Fairgrieve
John Francome
Miriam Francome

Guy Gluckstein
Yvonne Gilespie
Lt. Col. C.R.D. Gray
Frank Gilman

Alison Hancock
Sarah Hobbs
Ron Hyett
John Hislop
Tony Hide
John Halford
Lawrence Hyde
Ivor Herbert
Gavin Hunter
Bruce Hobbs
John Hume
Denis Haynes
Mrs T. Holland-Martin
David Harsent
Jane Halford
Hugh Hanby
David Harris
Dave Hanley

Jeremy Issacs

Bob Kemp
Kevin Kerr

Simon Lycett Green
Ursula Lockhart
E.P. Luke

Kelly Marks
Peter Michael
Elain Mellor
Mrs W. McAlpine
Freddie Maxwell
Mrs Joe Mercer
Bryan Marshall
Mrs Michael Marsh
Mrs E.M. Marshall
Doug Marks
Arthur Moore
Peter McKeever

David Nicholson
Dinah Nicholson
Mrs Pamela Normand
Major Patrick Ness

Peter O'Sullevan

Gavin Pritchard-Gordon
Douglas Pilkington
Major M.B. Pope
David Pilkington
Major Nick Peto
Bernard Parkin

Dick Peacock
"The Professor"
Angus Panton

John Rumble
Pat Rohan
The Earl of Ronaldshay
Mrs Timothy Riley
Lady Rootes
Jocelyn Reavey
Lord Ramsay
Gordon Richards

Arthur Sidey
Brough Scott
Ian Scott
Sheila Steele
Mrs Ron Smyth
Mrs Michael Stoute
Capt. Mark Smyly
Monica Sheriffe
Lt. Col. C.J. Sidgwick
Sue Skeen

A.W. Thompson
"Tot"
The Marchioness of
Tavistock
Tim Thomson Jones

C. Vincent
Fiona Vigors
C. Vernon Miller

Robert Winter
Peter Walwyn
Mrs Ron Ward
Andrew Wates
David Wickins
Waring Willis
Sir David Wills
John Webber

THE TRAINER'S 10 COMMANDMENTS

1
Thou shalt have no other gods but the gods in Portman Square.

2
Thou shalt not bow down nor worship any other, for the Stewards of the Jockey Club have been known to visit the sins of the fathers upon the children of the 3rd and 4th generations.

3
Thou shalt not bawl obscenities at thy stable lads sufficiently foul to shock their grandmothers.

4
Thou shalt work like a beaver for 6 days, but the assistant trainer can cope on the Sabbath.

5
Honour thy father and mother, and those of other trainers, for you're bound to be related to them one way or another.

6
Thou shalt not murder nor maim any interfering owner.

7
Thou shalt not commit adultery with thine owners' wives, and preferably not with thy secretary either.

8
Thou shalt not steal a march on the punters by keeping a stable full of dark horses.

9
Thou shalt not bear false witness at any inquiry, for others will surely do the same to you.

10
Thou shalt not covet the horses of other trainers, nor make any attempt to nobble them.

AND MAY THE GOOD LORD HAVE MERCY ON THE LOT OF YOU

AS MR. FRANCOME WAS SAYING

Some kids grow up in cabbage patches,
Erratically, in snitches and snatches.
Stewards are erratic too,
Think one thing—another do.
They'll tear a jockey apart, and then,
Erratically patch him together again.
Officers, gentlemen, public school snobs,
Old boys together, the toffs and the nobs.
Though cabbage patch stewards may be upper-class,
Their cabbage patch brains are remarkably sparse.

A titled young lady from Rayner
Had been for a ride with her trainer.
You could tell she'd been laid.
More than once, I'm afraid,
By the smile on the face of the trainer.

There was a jolly jockey once
Lived up 'Cester way.
He laughed and sang from morn 'til night.
No lark could be more gay.

And this the gist of what he sang,
Counting up his dough,
"I'll ride for anyone, any old where,
So long as it's quid pro quo."

OWNERS ON TRAINERS

Trainers, prone to repetition,
On failure never dwell.
Take the classic supposition—
Didn't he do well?

My horse was far from clever.
Unlikely to excel.
But when he ran, however—
Didn't he do well?

It didn't matter where he came,
Or even if he fell.
The phrase was always just the same—
Didn't he do well?

And when I hesitantly said,
"I think it's time to sell."
He made me buy two more instead—
Didn't he do well?!

TRAINERS ON OWNERS

The Owner is a necessary evil.
A time consuming blight.
He talks a lot of twaddle, but—
The Owner's always right.

He rings for information
In the middle of the night;
Objects to all your entries, for—
The Owner has the right.

You meet him in the Champagne Bar
And pay to get him tight.
He thinks he's got a winner, and—
Of course he thinks he's right.

And when his horse fades in the straight,
Or falls at the final flight,
He blames it all on you, because—
The Trainer's *never* right.

HOLLYWOOD PARTY   by Be My Guest
                                   out of Western Goddess

Here's a little proverb you surely ought to know.
Horses sweat and men perspire but ladies only glow.

A trainer was saddling a runner at Ayr.
The rain pouring down drenched the miserable pair.
The trainer was poor and his runner was thin,
Only a skeleton covered in skin.
The trainer nipped off for a jar and a snack.
He was but a moment, but when he got back,
His runner was gone, and in anguish he cried,
"Oh, where is my horse?" The stewards replied,
"Your horse, Sir, has drowned in a puddle.
Fell into a puddle and drowned.
The poor little thing was so thirsty and thin
She bent for a drink, and, sadly, fell in.
She's in Heaven, and perfectly happy.
She won't need a trainer no more.
Your horse, Sir, was drowned in a puddle.
Not lost, Sir, but gone on before."

HANDICAPPER BLUES

The head lad was angry; the secretary mad.
They couldn't believe the weights were so uncharitably bad.
"The handicapper's lost his head and all his marbles too,
He's shovelled every bit of lead upon our Saucy Sue."
The trainer went a pallid shade and screamed, "The man's insane!
He's done his level best to see she'll never run again."

The trainer called the office on his mobile, cordless phone,
And asked the handicapper in a more conciliatory tone,
"Please take a pound or two away, my horse is far too frail,
The weight allotted means her whole career you might curtail."

The trainer tried his very best with endless charming chatter,
But the handicapper said he was quite set upon the matter.
The owner didn't understand and wanted some more fun,
And swore he wouldn't pay the bills unless she had a run.
So run she did, with such a weight of very heavy metal,
The little horse collapsed and died—dead as a bloody nettle.

An ardent young trainer with upstanding member
Liked delicious young jockeys of feminine gender.
As expected, of course,
It was he, not the horse,
Who gave them the rides to remember.

A pretty young thing from Madras
Has a perfectly beautiful ass.
But not, as you'd think,
Firm, rounded and pink,
But grey, with pricked ears, and eats grass.

WELL RIGGED   by Windjammer
                                          out of Topless Dancer

MISS INDISCRETION   by Mr. Bigmore
                                            out of Office Party

CAUTIONARY TALE FOR TRAINERS

Lady owners are notorious
For falling in love with their trainers
When they are victorious.
It is a phenomenon I have noticed in the past,
And one, I can assure you, which doesn't last.
Luck, like salt, has a way of running out,
And lady owners, like rats, are pretty quick
On the old turn-about.
Before you can say, "Jack-bloomin'-Robinson"
She'll be out of your yard and into that of
Mr. Win-em-all Henderson.

MORAL
Do not assume you've got it made
Once the lady's laid,
For nothing so enjoyably improper
Could save you coming such a catastrophic cropper.

There was a crooked trainer
Who swopped a crooked horse
And they both went together
To a crooked little course.
They found a crooked jock
Who raced a crooked mile
And they all won together
A crooked little pile.

ROLL IN THE HAY   by Honest Pleasure
out of Court Barns

BOY GEORGE   by Music Boy
out of Zitzi Girl

CAPTAIN CRUMPET   by Home Guard
out of Farmer's Daughter

I have a horse who has perfected the extraordinary and frustrating art of never coming in any place, any time, any where, on any day . . . . but where he's going, there's no coming back!

WHO HE?

Please speak to me gently, without raising your voice, and without contradicting me in any way. In people of my age noise and contradiction provoke hypertension, gastric hyperacidity and cardio-vascular trouble, and we rapidly become disagreeable. Do not forget, please, that I am your Trainer, and, as such, require careful handling.

Royal Ascot is always so thrilling,
With ladies in flounces and frilling.
If the horses take fright
At an unstable sight
It's probably Mrs. G. Shilling.

The variations
In pronunciations
Make me feel a fool.
One that makes mock
Is Tim Forster's jock.
His name is not Hywel
It's Hule!

UNLIKELY   by Blandford
out of Lady Southampton

A stallion of adventurous disposition,
Although relishing variable coition,
Could not find a mare
Who would ever dare
Try the 69 position.

Some jockeys are Dads.
Some jockeys are Mums.
You can tell which is which
By the shape of their bums.

TOAST FROM A NEWLY WED JOCKEY TO HIS WIFE

May we live as long as we want to,
And, as long as we live, may we want to.
If I'm asleep and you want to—wake me.
If I don't want to—make me.

TRAINERS' EXCUSES AND OWNERS' THOUGHTS

He's a bit short of a run	(Tub of lard)
He didn't settle	(Neurotic)
Left-handed course didn't suit him	(Doubtful)
Right-handed course ditto	(Definitely doubtful)
Doesn't travel well	(Unadventurous)
Track was a bit tight	(Or jockey tight)
Needs the top of the ground	(Wait for a drought)
Likes the mud	(Wait for a flood)
The going was against him	(He's no swan)
Never galloped freely	(Not even a goose)
He was disappointing	(He's a bloody duck)
He's a bit lazy	(He's bone idle)
He got hemmed in	(Jockey needs a bollocking)
He was very unlucky	(Weren't we all)
He swallowed his tongue	(Wish I'd swallowed mine before I backed him each-way)
Might try blinkers next time	(Face facts, you've bought a camel)
Thought he would win until the final furlong	(He'd lost before he left the paddock)
Going well until the last	(Never stood a chance)
He'll strip fitter next time	(Trust in the power of prayer)
Hasn't found his form	(Shoot the bugger)

JOSH

Cricket's my sport, my summer delight,
And my amateur team is my joy.
But I'm strictly a pro when it comes to the nags.
I'm the Wizard of Findon, my boy.

TAX HAVEN by Quayside
            out of Money Please

BASIE   by Jazzeiro
            out of Orchestration

T'was said to me of Barry Hills
That he was fond of taking pills
To stop himself from getting fat.
Four for himself and four for his hat.
But, as the hat just grew and grew,
I feel this story can't be true.

The Marchioness of Tavistock admits,
"I love breeding horses.
It beats driving Porsches."

Phil Solomons said, when told his horse would
run like a real Christian, "I don't want him
to run like a Christian, I want him to run like
a Jew."

Horses are red.
Horses are blue.
Horses that lose
Are turned into glue.

                        USHERETTE by Coliseum
                            out of Follow Me.

LADIES LOO AT THE POINT-TO-POINT

Remember gloomy tents and muddy floors?
Unreachable, non-fastening doors?
Balancing precariously on slats
With shuffling feet and bobbing hats?
Shuddering at the awful breeze,
Belongings clasped upon our knees?
Today's improvement—mobile loos,
And never ending blasted queues.

An octogenarian lady owner was overheard discussing jockeys
and trainers with her nonagenarian lady friend. "They're a
pretty randy lot you know, Sybil. It must be all that bumping
up and down in the saddle. The condition is permanent I'm
told, dear. They may lose their marbles but never their
balls."

ADVICE TO AN OWNER

Your trainer tells a flattering tale,
Delusive, vain and hollow.
Let not your trainer's talk prevail,
Lest disappointment follow.

ADVICE TO A TRAINER

When your horses beat the field
When they should have lost, not won.
When the dope tests prove conclusive,
Chuck your licence in . . . . and run!

CASSANOVA'S STORY   by Immortal Love
out of Havelotte

CREMATION   by Ashmore
out of Sacred Ibis

PUNTER'S LAMENT

My semi-detached went to Mecca.
My Cortina to William Hill.
My children's bright prospects have clouded,
Their legacies paid Ladbroke's bill.
My friends showered me with compassion
And advice to arrest my fall.
Then my wife ran away with a bookie,
Which just shows you can't lose them all.

Clive Graham once wrote that the form book should have been
written in Braille for the benefit of the Stewards.

ON BUYING A HORSE

One white foot, try him.
Two white feet, buy him.
Three white feet, put him in the dray.
Four white feet, give him away.
Four white feet and a white nose,
Take off his hide and feed him to the crows.

In 1874, the Nawab of Bahawalpore started a horse breeding
establishment. Having seen a horse called Recovery running
at Mooltan Races, he offered the owner 15 hundred rupees for
him as a resident stallion. As the owner had only given 300
rupees for him, the offer was promptly accepted. Recovery
went to the Bahawalpore Stud where he caused much
disappointment by refusing to perform his duties. A closer
examination proved him to be a gelding.

SCALDED   by Hotfoot
            out of Quick Burn

A good horse should have three properties of a man; three of a woman; three of a fox; three of a hare and three of an ass.

Of a man — Bold. Proud. Hardy.
Of a woman— Fair-breasted. Bright of hair. Easy mover.
Of a fox — Fair tail. Short ears. Good trot.
Of a hare — Great eye. Dry head. Well running.
Of an ass — Big chin. Flat leg. Good hoof.

A horse with only one testicle is known as a 'rig'.
David Barons once trained one called 'Something's Missing'.

When Mrs Rimell wears a hat
Of corduroy or mink,
She has an air of majesty
I very often think.
And though her name is Mercy
It's merciful she's not.
When it comes to training horses
She's as hard as Brighton rock.
But when she takes her hat off,
It's really quite uncanny,
Her grey hair proves, without a doubt,
She's just a nice, old granny.

FRENCH CREAM   by Faubourg
out of Nivea

SWEET SONNET   by Honeyway
out of Verse

FRANCOME (MR)

He had such long and curly hair
That surely it was hardly fair
To get so cross when not called "Mr"?
We think, they thought he was his sister!

A pretty young jockette, Lyn Inkers,
Emptied the bar at the racecourse of drinkers.
For while jumping the first,
Her brassiere burst,
And her horse got a warm pair of blinkers.

COHABITING   by Homing
out of Bedfellow

UNLIKELY STORY

Steve was a jump jockey, sexy and bright,
With a most gargantuan appetite.
He had blondes for breakfast, lunch and tea,
And for dinner, another two or three.
But the years advanced, and his eyes so big
Grew hungrier far than his thingummyjig.
So now, poor chap, he has to make do
With just the occasional one or two.

DOM PERIGNON   by Sparkler
                out of Breathalyser

Newmarket gossip just thrives.
It's a wonder a person survives.
There are lunches and dinners
For losers and winners
While the chaps play around with the wives.

This typical, over-weight, landed lord
Goes to the races because he's bored.
Hail-fellow-well-met in the Champagne Bar,
He gesticulates with a large cigar,
While 'neath his Trilby hat there glows
An aristocratic, mulberry nose.

His whiskery ears might catch a tip
The well-informed allow to slip.
Leaving his glass, he rushes out
Sure it's the winner he's dreamed about.
As the noble lord hoves into sight,
His bookie smiles, as well he might—

The bet his lordship's bound to lose
Will pay for his Mediterranean cruise.

HOW'S YOUR HORSE?

If people ask me,
I invariably reply,
"He's coming to hand nicely,
Thank you,
I'm very pleased so say.
No, he won't be running in the Derby,
But he may pop down to Bath.
He's coming to hand nicely,
Thank you,
In the most encouraging way."

If people inquire,
I always tell them,
"He ran very well,
Thank you,
I'm very glad to say.
No, he didn't actually win this time.
No, he didn't quite make the frame.
But he ran very well,
Thank you.
He wasn't disgraced today."

A jockey they called, Mac The Knife,
Had a marvellously active young wife.
As he straddled her thighs,
Crying, "Rise, Madam, rise,"
She would give him the ride of his life.

Said Oaksey, "It's chances are none,"
Before the big race had begun.
"It's jumping's so bad,
If you back it, you're mad."
And it romped home at twenty to one.

MAROONED   by Mill Reef
            out of Short Rations

There was an amorous owner,
Whose name I will not repeat,
Whose affair with his trainer's wife
Was blatant and indiscreet.
Unable to leave her alone
He followed her everywhere
Until in *The Sporting Life*
They mentioned the matter there.
The trainer saw and swore aloud,
"What's sauce for the bloody goose
Is sauce for this old gander . . . .
I, too, can play fast and loose."

And thus the naughty couple
Were hoist by their own petard.
Now the trainer lives in the manor house
While the owner mucks out in the yard.

FLYING FISHNET   by Charlottesville Flyer
                 out of Black Stocking

Between Findon and Ayr one day,
A horse box was well on its way.
The horse in the back
Was a big, rangy black,
But they should have been taking the grey.

In the 19th century it was thought desirable for owners of horses in the damp climate of the British Isles to supply their stables with heat. Open fires burning wood or coal were considered the most effective method. Lieut-Gen. Sir F. Fitzwilliam, Bart., wrote, "There is really no good reason why the owner of valuable horses should grudge the expense of an open fireplace in the stable. The horses will gain in health and condition far more than is counterbalanced by the trifling extra cost."

HOW DOTH THE CUNNING TRAINER

How doth the cunning trainer
Improve his average string?
Insuring he can gain the
Riches of a king.

How he'll simper, how he'll grin
At rich and pompous bores.
And welcome lady owners in
With gently smiling jaws.

Gavin, old chap, entre nous,
Since you can't be disturbed on the loo.
A portable phone
While you sit there alone,
Might solve this small problem for you.

In the racing world the gentlemanly rule is, that all
            sinners shall be nameless.
For no names, no pack drill, means that everyone is
            blameless.
Which is all right on the night, but not in the early
            morning after
When you're in the right bed, with the wrong wife, and
            your human alarm clock–or, more precisely,
            your assistant trainer, is standing there
            shaking with laughter.
            And guess why?

            The sod's a spy–
            For *Private Eye*.

DANGER AHEAD by Mill Reef
              out of Land Ho

COURT GOSSIP   by Imperial Fling
               out of Babble On

THE UPSTART   by Status Seeker
               out of Lady Harford

There was a once common practice of inserting powdered ginger under a horse's tail to give it temporary spirit– hence, to ginger up a bit.

Now Simon Green once had a horse
That ran on Fundador.
It's trainer used the self-same fuel,
But swallowed rather more.
They won the Arc de Triomphe,
The Guineas and the Oaks.
The punters, they had never known,
Such profitable soaks.
From five to fifty furlongs
The ageless racer flew,
As though her steps were guided
By some enchanted brew.
But Simon, tired of winning,
And weary of the sham,
Closed the secret pipeline
From Spain to Middleham.
Now from horse and trainer
The public gaze has fled.
Too thirsty to be running.
Too pickled to be dead.

RULES FOR PUNTERS

A good horse
A good jockey

A good bet

A good horse
A poor jockey

A moderate bet

A moderate horse
A good jockey

A moderate bet

A bad horse
A poor jockey

No bet

There's a filly I ride over fences
Who jumps well—could I ask for more?
But the filly who gives me the best ride
Is the wife of the fellow next door.

I worked for trainer Malone.
Wore my fingers to the bone.
But when I asked for £1 more
You should have heard him moan.
And, though his owners pay a bomb,
I'm sure you will agree,
He could dispose of his four wheels
And bike about like me.

But, I've never seen a trainer on a bike.
No. I've never seen a trainer on a bike.
Wherever I've been, I never miss a thing,
And, I've never seen a trainer on a bike.

Said a jockey with bitter remorse
As he legged it in from the course,
"I know I showed flair
As I flew through the air.
If only I'd taken the horse."

Some are known by the clothes they wear.
Take The Duke, with his coat like a bear.
He gives people shocks
With his bright scarlet socks,
Which he buys by the gross, not the pair.

Re-opening the tea room door,
I nearly fainted on the floor.
It could not possibly be
The Duke would pay for two for tea?
There must have been a grave mistake
To pay for sandwiches and cake.
The thought that he would part with cash
Did seem, for him, a trifle rash.
But all my queries proved it right,
The Duke is really not so tight.

JOCKEY'S MOAN

They call me small, 'cos I'm not very tall.
Always near a phone when a trainer may call.
In order to ride his bloody trials
I drive my car thousands of miles.

MORE MOAN

When a jockey has to starve and sweat.
Goes to the course and gets soaking wet.
Gets beat on the fav'rite, the flying grey.
You must admit that's one helluva day.

He's a real Percy Thrower
With his sit-upon mower,
A gift from his punter in Leeds.
A few lost races
And misjudged paces
Have done well for his gardening needs.

OUR GRACIE   by Star Appeal
                    out of Tinkling Sound

COLONIAL CARESS   by Dominion
                    out of Buss

Lord, give me pluck to jump a fence
So big, that even I,
When boasting of it to my friends,
Shall have no need to lie.

There's only one thing that makes a man look a bigger bloody fool than a horse—and that's a woman.

THE BUMPER

He looks an ass.
His talk is crass.
He wears an old school tie.
His style is crude.
His tactics rude.
His finish makes one sigh.
But on the day,
Cash bet, away,
He bleeds the bookies dry.

A colt, rather randy, went racing.
Just hurdling, rather than chasing.
But the size of his dong
Was so long and so strong
It imperilled his ultimate placing.

A jockey is a lovesome thing, God wot!
Short; squat;
Lean shins;
Misbegot;
An oddity though bright. And yet, the fool contends
That God is not.
Not God! Upon the Turf! When the favourite wins?
Nay, if winnings are the test,
Sure t'was God who beat the rest.

STEAL THE SHOW   by Comedy Star
                        out of Main Chance

THE UNDERGRADUATE   by Scallywag
                        out of Miss Cantab

Two things I know about a horse
And one of them is rather coarse.

The Trainer asked
The Princess.
The Princess said,
"Of course not.
You'll never lose that over-weight
If you go on eating bread."
The Trainer asked
His missus
Who said, "It is
A certainty.
Why not eat an apple now
And when you go to bed?"
The Trainer said,
"I'll ask Her."
And went to see
Her Highness.
He bowed to Her Highness
And went a little red.
"Excuse me,
Your Highness,
For asking quite
So frequently,
But could I take an apple
As a substitute for bread?"
The Princess snapped,
"Of course not.
You mustn't eat
A single thing,
And don't attempt to take a jar
Of whisky-mac instead."
The Trainer went
A whiter shade,
And looked a
Piteous sight.
But, "If you suggest nothing . . . .
I'll take nothing, ma'am," he said.
The Princess told,
The Trainer,
"I think you're
Bloody marvellous."
The Trainer paused a moment, then,
"That's two of us," he said.

A young trainer's wife composed in the loo
Limericks rude, and libellous too.
She sat there all day and into the night
'Til her husband got shirty and put out the light.
He remarked, with a pout, "I presume that you do,
Between making up rhymes, still indulge in a screw?"

The lady called out through the half-open door,
"Can we possibly do it by semaphore?
I couldn't stop now, my rhyme's incomplete,
And it's far too alarmingly indiscreet.
Don't worry," she added, "There's plenty of time.
Thank God, at your age, you're still in your prime."

Back came the cry, "You'd better watch out,
Or I'll soon become rusty and horribly stout."
But the lady knew better, and later that night,
She conclusively proved she was perfectly right.

PETER McKEEVER'S GOAT

Now Peter McKeever was an Irishman of note,
And one day, at the North Wall, he tried to shift a goat
Which had a mind to travel with it's equine friend that day.
And the question for McKeever–should it go or should it stay?

The goat was quite determined that it was going to sail,
And threatenings and cajolings were just to no avail.
When McKeever had the notion he would get it off the boat,
He underestimated the devotion of the goat.

With a grandeur that was worthy of it's relative King Puck,
It resisted every effort to make it come unstuck.
But time was quickly passing–the officials were irate.
They couldn't wait much longer as the boat was very late.

They rang the English trainer who eventually said
That he'd accept the animal when it came to Holyhead.
And so the goat had won the day – it's plans no-one could foil.
And they granted it a licence to land on British soil.

SPICE MARKET   by Native Bazaar
                       out of Mustard Flower

A little neglect may breed mischief; for want of a nail, the shoe was lost; for want of a shoe, the horse was lost; for want of a horse, the rider was lost.

Seen on a bookie's tombstone . . . 'Heads I win.
Tails you lose.'

SEA PARROT   by Ocean Swell
                    out of Precious Polly

"NAVICULAR JOE"

I'm only a selling 'chaser,
Bandaged, bow tendoned and thin.
I like courses like Bangor and Cartmel,
Because there I'm more likely to win.

I admit that the races I run in,
Are races that aren't run too fast.
But not once in my life have I fallen.
Not once in my life have come last.

Each season my way has been paid for.
Have a bet on me, I'll have a go.
With my lungs fit to burst,
I just love to come first,
And I've never been claimed,
'Cos I'm constantly lame . . .
And my name . . . it's "Navicular Joe".

The rich taxed racehorse owner leaves the poor taxed trainer to manage his over taxed horses and allows a small taxed jockey to ride them for a taxed fee with taxed tack on heavily taxed race courses, paying tax again for the privilege.

Lord, but gambling's a rum show to deal with
As Curley found to his cost.
And I reckon it's just through the gambling
The last man on earth'll be lost.

FASCINATING TRICK   by Buckpasser
out of Intriguing

ROYAL DILEMMA   by Buckpasser
out of Queen Empress

WORDS FROM A TRAINER

Now, this is the Law of The Club,
As ancient as God's universe.
If you keep it, you surely will prosper.
If you break it, you'll go in reverse.

Cringe daily from nose-tip to tail-tip;
Bow deeply, and grovel, and squirm;
Say, 'Yes, Sir' and 'No, Sir' and 'Please Sir',
But, on no account let the worm turn.

Ride your horse past the post 'till he drops,
But not too much whip, they insist.
If you ease him, they say you're not trying.
No injections—they'll get you dismissed.

If by chance you get called to the Square,
And your thoughts are all gloomy and black.
Just remember the port they have there,
And the cardinal rule—Don't Talk Back.

ARTIST'S PROOF   by Gainsborough
                   out of Clear Evidence

ART PAPER   by Artist's Proof
                   out of Quire

When naïve jockey stoops to folly,
And finds too late that men betray.
What bribes can ease his melancholy?
What fines can wash his guilt away?

Newmarket is like a stable full of fed horses . . . everyone neighs
after his neighbour's wife.

Billy is a punter.
What a silly Billy!
Went and put a monkey on
An untried filly.

The filly was as green
As a young brussel sprout.
Billy lost his money
And was all cleaned out.

He sobbed into his race card.
He sobbed into his port.
The bookies grinned from ear to ear
And said he was a sport.

They told him he was lucky.
Told him never to despair.
Promised him the earth and said
He'd be a millionaire.

They offered endless credit.
Said he'd surely win somehow.
But Billy went on losing . . .
. . . Guess who's sobbing now?

ADVICE TO THE WIFE OF AN AMATEUR RIDER – PERHAPS?

He will hold thee, when his passion shall have spent it's novel force,
Something better than his dog – a little dearer than his horse.

THE PROS AND CONS OF A.I. WITH THE THOROUGHBRED

Nobody asked the mares. But the mares asked the cows and
ALL the cows were of the opinion that . . .

The farmyard is not much fun, Sir.
The meadows are not very gay.
When the one bit of fun, in the year's dismal run
Has, by science, been taken away.

If used to be fun in the meadows.
We looked forward to what was in store.
The cowslip in flower–the bullrush–what power.
But now all we get is a straw.
What style we showed in the pastures.
We kept the old bull on the run.
There were forty of us, but, without any fuss,
We conceived with immeasurable fun.

But science has altered the pattern.
For the bull, and the cow, life's a bore.
The twain shall not meet, so the sexual feat
Is that liquid, nitrogenous straw.

You humans may laugh at our prattle.
You may scorn all the things that we say.
But it isn't a joke. We just long for a poke,
Like you . . . in the old fashioned way.

TREACHERY   by Flag of Truce
            out of Snake River

As a bookie, Sir, I've studied men,
And find this to be true.
Some are honest. Others rotten.
But most between the two.

A jump jockey hailing from Wales
Had habits unlike other males,
For he frequently skewered
The Stipendary Steward,
And pleasured the Clerk of the Scales.

TONGUE TIED MUSE   by Stage Door Johnny
                         out of Constant Nymph

Some may call it sneaking.
Others, telling tales.
But Scu was right to protest
When Tate missed out the scales.

He'd won the race by three lengths
Through the January mud,
But the stewards took it off him
While the punters screamed for blood.

Les Kennard said, "I'm sorry,
I hate to win this way.
But rules are rules, old fella,
Even amateurs must obey."

Poor Thomas, he was furious,
And threw down all his tack.
"My first time at Worcester,
And I'm never coming back."

CHELTENHAM NATIONAL HUNT MEETING

Just look around you at the crowd,
Some dressed smartly, some so loud.
Our dear Queen Mum is dressed in pink,
And Mercy's in *another* mink.
There's Hermes scarves and hats from Scotts,
And there's the Duke in scarlet socks.
We've had the picnic, drunk the wine,
And luckily the weather's fine.
The place is full of friends who've come
From far and wide to share the fun
On this the very gem of courses,
Betting on the best of horses . . . .
Hurdlers; chasers; even hunters.
A glorious heyday for us punters.
Win—or lose—"Vive le sport."
Next March we'll all be back for more.

Pat Rohan is quite convinced that—

"North, South, East and West,
Rohan's horses are the best."

ROADBLOCK   by Warpath
                     out of Speed Trap

MUSICAL PUSS   by Orchestra
                      out of Cool Kitten

Gentlemen love lady jockeys.
It could be the boots, or the whips.
When I'm dressed in my gear
They all ogle and leer—
But I know they're just after my tips!

WHAT A SHAME

The Duke pulled off a double,
And so did jockey Scu.
What made it more remarkable,
The owner had one too.

Comedian and Little Sloop,
The brown horse and the bay,
Were winners at Wincanton
On the very self-same day.

But no one took a picture.
The owner's scrapbook's bare.
No photographs to paste in . . .
The photographers weren't there!

HORSE POWER – Mr. Watt calculated that a good, strong dray horse, working at a gin for eight hours a day, averaged 22,000 foot pounds per minute. He increased this by 50%, and this has been the recognised unit of power measurement ever since.

There was an entire from Larkhill
Who swallowed an atom bomb pill.
His genital organ
Was found in Glamorgan.
His balls on a bush in Brazil.

MR. BRAMWELL
(Written by Denis Haynes in 1983)

My name is Michael 'Bramal'. I *am* the National Stud.
I run it by committee, as God decreed I should.
They really are quite decent chaps, of that there is no doubt,
And if one ever interfered, I'd have the bugger out.
The stallions are our centrepiece, and though they're bloody good,
Be under no delusions, Sir, *I* am the National Stud.

There's a certain Northern jockey
Who, with quite a lot of force,
Is inclined to come to Redcar and
To criticise our Course.

If it isn't the rough going
Or the sharpness of the bends,
It's the lack of decent sandwiches—
So, we've tried to make amends.

We've built up both the cambers
And put in hand repairs.
The bends now ride like walls of death
Seen at country fairs.

We've taken on the catering,
Specifically to see
That this great figure of the Turf
Receives a proper tea.

We've modernised the Jockeys' Room,
(You should have seen the bill!)
And laid down carpet for his feet
So he'll not catch a chill.

And if, next year, he still complains,
Our efforts he refutes,
We'll fix him up a special peg
On which to hang his boots!

Mrs Normand suggests:-
If at first you have a sinner,
Be patient 'til she breeds a winner.

Doug Marks comments:-
Had I worried less
That I would breathe my last,
What joy I would have missed
When the danger passed.

HARD TACK by Hard Sauce
          out of Cowes

Hello, Josh, if you're willing,
I might, without killing
Myself, make it right down to Cheltenham.
I hope that your jockey
Is not playing hockey,
And I don't like the one who keeps belting him.
He's a sensitive horse,
And I feel that the course
Is not one that I'd personally choose.
But, since you insist
That he go on the list,
On your head—should he happen to lose.

Lady Rootes – how delightful.
I'm sure nothing frightful
Will happen to cause you dismay.
But I feel you should know
You can't have Richard Rowe
As I've entered six horses that day.
I've three in the first,
And, as yours is the worst,
You'll have to make do with the 'prentice.
I fear – though they oughter –
They won't make the water,
And the lad will end up at the dentist!

Ride on the two-legged mare—you're swinging from the gallows.

Ride on a horse with ten toes—you're walking.

With envious eyes I turn and stare
Convinced that life is hardly fair.
There she stands on the Ascot course
My old school chum with her winning horse.
At school she was hopeless at every game,
A dunce at work and extremely plain.
But now she's blonde and often wed.
"She succeeds on her back". I've heard it said.
My envy boils over—the mink-clad bitch.
I'd like to put her nose in a twitch.
She pats her horse; plays coy with the Press;
One more click and she might undress.
Perhaps I'd better change my ways,
No matter what my mother says,
For surely I could play her game—
Crumbs! She's waving! Suggesting champagne!
Of course, with a smile, I quickly accept,
For into my mind a thought has crept.
With a word of advice from such a winner
I, too, could be a successful sinner.

The Jockey Club is the true embodiment
Of everything that's excellent.
It has no kind of fault or flaw.
In short, more perfect than the Law.
(And like the Law, an ass.)

45

An over-sexed jockey named Reg
Was laying a lass in a hedge.
Along came his wife
With a razor-sharp knife
And cut off his joint and two veg.

TRICKY BUSINESS   by Tycoon
out of Gay Tricks

When I see a trainer over polite to his owners' friends; begging them to indulge in yet more champagne at his expense; over playing the role of modesty whilst nonchalantly letting it be known that no one can train horses as miraculously as he . . . then thinks I, "That man has a horse to sell."

I am tall and rather stately,
And I care not very greatly
What you say, or what you do.
I'm Henry—who are you?

ROAST DUCK by Sea Bird
out of Clinkers

A handsome young jockey lay dying,
And, as on the green turf he lay,
To the stewards who round him came sighing,
These last dying words he did say.

"Take my saddle, my girth and my stirrups;
Hang my boots up; knot up my rein;
Take my whip, my helmet and goggles,
And toast my demise in champagne."

47

JOAN OF ARC	by Never Say Die out of Freedom
GOLDEN HANDSHAKE	by Golden Cloud out of For Nothing
GODDESS	by Immortality out of Virtuous
JUNGLE DRUM	by Delirium out of Message
BRIGHT and BREEZY	by Set Fair out of Sea Air
BOLOGNESE	by Zucchero out of Spaghetti
SATAN'S SLIDE	by Precipitation out of Hell's Fury
PILLOW FIGHT	by Combat out of Wagon-Lit
TORY VICTORY	by Bright News out of Fair Freedom
NIGHT VISITOR	by What a Guest out of Naughty Lass

Special thanks to   Sally Cook
Miriam Francome
Elain Mellor
Dinah Nicholson
Meg Radbourne
Fiona Vigors

Published by Beenham House Publications
© Copyright SIA

Design donated by Gordon House
Printed in England by THE MIDAS PRESS